Dealing with Fee

Caring

Isabel Thomas

Illustrated by Clare Elsom

Raintree

Raintree is an imprint of Capstone Global Library
Limited, a company incorporated in England and
Wales having its registered office at 7 Pilgrim Street,
London, EC4V 6LB – Registered company number:
6695582

www.raintreepublishers.co.uk
myorders@raintreepublishers.co.uk

Text © Capstone Global Library Limited 2013
First published in hardback in 2013
Paperback edition first published in 2014
The moral rights of the proprietor have
been asserted.

Edited by Dan Nunn, Rebecca Rissman, and
 Catherine Veitch
Designed by Philippa Jenkins
Original illustrations © Clare Elsom
Illustrated by Clare Elsom
Production by Victoria Fitzgerald
Originated by Capstone Global Library Ltd
Printed and bound in China

ISBN 978 1 406 25038 1 (hardback)
16 15 14 13 12
10 9 8 7 6 5 4 3 2 1

ISBN 978 1 406 25048 0 (paperback)
17 16 15 14
10 9 8 7 6 5 4 3 2 1

**British Library Cataloguing in Publication
Data**
Thomas, Isabel.
Caring. -- (Dealing with Feeling...)
152.4'1-dc23
A full catalogue record for this book is available from
the British Library.

Contents

Some words are shown in bold, **like this**. Find out what they mean in the glossary on page 23.

What does being caring mean?

Everybody has **feelings**. Being caring means that you care about other people's feelings.

Caring people like to help other people feel good. People show they care when they help other people.

What does it feel like to be caring?

Caring people feel bad when someone else is sad, angry, worried, or lonely. They try to help people feel better.

Helping people to feel good makes you feel good, too. Being caring also helps you to make new friends.

How can I be caring?

You can be caring every day. Look for ways to help other people.

Caring people know when things are fair or unfair. They do their best to make things fair.

How do rules help me to be caring?

A caring person knows that rules help to make things fair for everyone. You can be caring by **obeying** rules.

You can be caring by helping with **housework,** even when it is not your turn. Being caring means thinking about what will make other people happy.

How can I help my friends to feel happy?

What do you do when your friends are sad or worried? Caring people make time to listen to their friends.

Be a good listener by asking questions. Look at people when they speak, and don't **interrupt**.

How can I help other people to feel happy?

Imagine that a new child joins your class. The child might be sad, scared, or shy.

You can be caring by speaking to them. A caring person makes sure that nobody feels left out.

What if I get mad at someone?

It is okay to feel angry sometimes. Thinking about how the other person feels will make you feel better. Perhaps the person did not mean to upset you.

Caring people say sorry when they have been unkind to somebody. Being caring means being **forgiving.**

What should I do if someone is not being caring?

Being caring means doing the right thing. If you see someone being unkind, the right thing to do is to tell a grown-up.

You can help by being kind to children who have been **bullied**. A caring person does not tease or bully people.

How can being caring make me happy?

Caring people are good friends to have. They are there when you need them.

If you are caring and helpful, people will share things with you. Being a good friend will help you to feel happy, too!

Make a caring toolbox

Write down some tips to help you care for others.

Notice when someone else is sad, angry, worried, or lonely.

Be a good listener.

Share and wait your turn.

Tell a grown-up if you see someone being unkind.

Include other people in your games.

Be friendly to children you don't know.

Look for ways to help people.

Think about what makes other people happy.

Glossary

bullied to be harmed or made fun of by somebody

feeling something that happens inside our minds. It can affect our bodies and the way we behave.

forgiving stop being angry with someone who has upset you

housework jobs that need to be done around your home

imagine make a picture in your head

interrupt stop somebody who is speaking by starting to speak yourself

obeying doing what a rule or grown-up says you are supposed to do

Find out more

Books

A Sick Day for Amos McGee, Philip Stead
   (First Second, 2012)

All Kinds of Feelings: A Lift-the-Flap Book,
   Emma Brownjohn (Tango Books, 2003)

I Want a Friend, Tony Ross (HarperCollins
   Children's Books, 2007)

Websites

bbc.co.uk/scotland/education/health/feelings

kidshealth.org/kid/feeling

pbskids.org/arthur/games/aboutface

Index